The Life of Trees ™

WRITTEN AND ILLUSTRATED BY DANIEL PRESEDO

special thanks:

Alicia Burstein, my rock.
Kai for keeping me young.
Eve for keeping me busy.

I support
life.

All kinds of
life.

Big and
small,
creepy and
crawly.

From a vibrant swamp.

To an
inhospitable
desert.

I thrive in lush rain forests –

I live High up
in the
mountains –

And that is
not all...

I can be elegant and fancy with the right care.

Or left alone to grow
super big and tall!

I am also content to
stay very small.

what kind of tree am I?

Are you hungry? I can make food for you.

what other foods grow on trees?

when it is
cold –

I help to provide warmth!

most days I just
soak it all in and
provide you oxygen!

I can be your
playground.

Build your
hideout!

Or your favorite chair.

But I grow
strong again!

Trees have been around for more than 370 million years.

Look around where you live.

what trees are around you?

share your inspired
tree art with us.

Twitter or
Instagram
@dramenon